They Clasp My Hand

They Clasp My Hand

A Family Memoir as Told in Poems

Elisabeth Frischauf

Published 2024
Printed in the United States of America
Print ISBN: 979-8-9908009-0-8
E-book ISBN: 979-8-9908009-1-5
Library of Congress Control Number: 2024912299

Cover and interior design by Tabitha Lahr
Front cover mixed media artwork by Elisabeth Frischauf
Back cover image © Shutterstock.com

For all my friends and family
and to refugees everywhere

Contents

***Prologue:* Song Bursts Forth**

Epigraph 3
My Holocaust 5
Legacy of the Horrific Times 8
Late Harvest 16
From Ashes 20
First Generation American 22
Around My Heart, A Vise 24
Haunted 26
I Own Tears for Everyone 31
Rootlings 34
Suddenly Torrents of Song 36
Postscript: *Never Again!* 37

***Part I All Over:* They Clasp My Hand**

The Call 41
Grief Swallows 45
A Hard Man to Love 48

Save Everything 51

Delve Deeper. 55

Revenge 60

Up the Ladder 65

Doors Open. Doors Close 66

Baltimore 71

Sorting Fragments 75

When Ma Dies 78

Pa's Cancer 81

Ma's Secrets. 83

Sunday Dinner. 86

1956, Our First Trip Home 88

The Chandelier 92

Ma's Slim Black-Lacquered

    Bookcases 95

The Letters 97

Mutti's Letters. 98

Holes 101

Any Other Day 102

Klara and Edith's Letters. 104

Papa's Letters 105
Miscellaneous Letters 107
All Over 109

Part II Crisscross Runways:
Kennedy/Schwechat/Kennedy

To Vienna 113
Game of Parts 115
Boxes 120
Hail the 1st of May 2019 121
May Fifth 123
Mother's Day, May 12, 2019 124
Goodbye, Danube River 127
Return to the _Landhaus_ 128
Later 131
My Grandson Waits 132

Acknowledgments 135
About the Author 137

Prologue:

Song Bursts Forth

Epigraph

Scattered Seeds

Seeds flowed over the sea
With sorrow and suffering.
Life resumes
Young leaves
Forced from mourning and misery
Take root in America's earth.

My Holocaust

Mine is a holocaust survivor family,
huddled on our life raft—the New World children.
Hope, driven by loss.

But this is not why my mother and father fled to America.
Here, we should not sorrow
yet that ever-present hole
gapes and yaws—
vicious maw ready to devour us.

So much pain, torment, endurance cracked.
Tossed aside—"organic waste matter"
(skin from the murdered useful for lampshades).
Grotesque German efficiency. This happened
to millions. And millions.

People *nothinged.*
Alive in the wrong place
at the wrong time
obscene yellow star on their sleeve.

And caught between, both grandmothers

Elisabeth Frischauf   5

swallowed in a mass grave.
Lost to us except in photographs
silent stares, vacant patches
in my mother's eyes,
my father's hands,
my parents' sudden, lowered voices.

Bleached, shadow-elders framed
in black on my mother's vanity.
Stare, clear-eyed. Unfamiliar.

Tell me, who are you?
Where do I continue?
Tell me, *Am I like Grossmutter Klara?*
Her name, my middle name.
Have I her eyes, her breasts, the corner of her nose?

Tears stun me—victim myself?
Klara herded naked into the *disinfecting shower*,
raining Zyklon B.
Gasping, asphyxiated, tossed into a heap of bodies,
picked over
for gold teeth and then,
burned to cinders in Auschwitz.

Grossmutter Edith carefully saved enough sleeping pills.
Her open Bible slipped softly into her lap,

my mother's photograph her last floating image.
Later boots stomped up the stairs. Smashed the front door—
the servants of the death machine find her slumped body,
denied its demise in a *home for old Jews.*

Never did my mother look at me and say,
>   *I remember when she laughed, her forehead wrinkled*
>   *just like yours!*

I remain, stranger in this here-and-before land
follow currents, washing over spellbound days.
I roll in feathered Hudson River clouds,
my bright body shining with orgasms and chocolate
    a loose sound . . .
            the shadows
                    fall. . . .

LEGACY OF THE HORRIFIC TIMES

Great-Uncle Hermann

I was told, he was tall, elegant, slim, rucksack on his back.
A pioneer in the new discipline of child psychiatry,
he made his medical rounds on a beat-up old bicycle.

Great-Uncle Hermann, imprisoned in Siberia.
casualty of World War I and
the collapsed Austro-Hungarian Empire.

I was told he walked home to Vienna.
Arrived hollow
no longer certain; Hope . . .

How did he do it?
Swallowed deep in his throat, haunting machine gun stutter
muffled screams, fog-cloud steps that made no noise—
He wrote poems.

From the last one, "Fragmente":

>. . . ich bin tausendmal anders
>Und nun steh' ich vor meinen Bruchstücken
>Alles ist nicht mehr.

Wenn du mich liebst, errätst du, was verloren
gegangen ist . . .

Fragments
 . . . I am a thousand times changed.
And so I stand before my splinters
Everything is no more.
If you love me, you will know what is lost . . .

Hermann died of TB in 1942,
contracted in Buchenwald.
A christened Lutheran, atheist, prisoner a second time.

All day I forget myself
back and forth, alive, lost.
Walk the broken pieces with him.

Great-Aunt Mitzi

From within Lager Gurs, Great-Aunt Mitzi writes
through barbed wire:

Lager Gurs, 1940

Ein anderer sinnloser Tag
Ein anderes leeres Blatt
Fiel aus dem Buch unseres Leben.

Another meaningless day
Another empty page
Fell from the book of our lives.

and

Ende März 1941

Oh, wie elend vergass ich
Die Bewegung des Frühlings
In dem eisigen Kummer
Dieses entzetzlichen Jahrs!

End of March 1941

Oh, in my misery, I forgot
The movement of Spring
In the icy sorrow
Of this appalling year!

Spring brings Mitzi to Mexico and, years later, she returns
to Vienna.
When I am nine, we meet. And once more,
when I'm nineteen, shortly before she dies.

Mama

Blueblack, bloodred ropes knot us—
I struggle, my crumpled baby-wings tear as they spread.

"Mama, a Monarch butterfly sat still on my finger!"
    Oh, our picnics by the Vienna woods. Clouds of buttercups,
    butterflies, meadowlarks, safe grass . . .
She talks to me. At me.

"But, Mama. . . ." She ignores me. I defer.
Cover myself in cool protection—
it's rare enough when she reveals a piece of her life.

"Mama, am I not your joy?"
    You destroy me with your demands, daughter.
My breasts bud, my first period. I sneak over to her
three-mirrored vanity.
Hmm, blue or green eyeshadow for my complexion?

    Stop at once. You will become vain. We can't have that.
She said she was out shopping! Beet red, I retreat,
learn to shut myself in my room and pull away.

She flings at me,
    You don't love me. I'll kill myself!
This dagger of hers, lightning strike to my core.

Mama, you tried and tried, told me you never had the money
to bring your mother safe to us in New York.

And then, the day when the Gestapo was to come for her—
kick her thin, hungry ribs, drag her fine gold hair,
to a stacked *standing room* only train car

no food, water, only a bucket for everyone's pee, shit
and vomit, hours of clack-clackity tracks, moans, sobs.
Shoves into the gas chamber and Mengele's *bakery*.

Mama, she decided to deny them. She swallowed
all the barbital in the pretty crystal bottle, labeled Veronal,
extinguished her life force
your face swimming beneath her sinking lids.

"No, Mama, you must NOT!"

When can I get the hell out of here?
Who can I be when I go out tonight?
Ruby-rose lipstick, patent leather pumps, my first date.

You won't miss me when I'm dead, Mama screams
through the closing front door.

She lived long enough to close the circle of her nightmare.
Through her bedroom window, ninety and blind,
she hears a plane buzz low over Broadway on crystal blue 9/11:
This sounds like Anschluss.

Papa

Behind his delight reciting Ogden Nash:
The trouble with a kitten is that/ eventually it becomes
a cat. . . .
A sudden blare. Out of nowhere.

Kristallnacht. We sit by his desk, radio set to WQXR.
The announcer speaks of remembering. Forgetting.
Papa cuts in, his flat, these-are-the-facts voice:
My mother was murdered in Auschwitz. She wouldn't
leave her sister.

He gets up and smiles at me,
Let's have some cake and coffee with your mother,
shall we?

Forty years old. First time I hear THIS!
Dumbstruck, I follow his short, rapid steps to join Mama
in the dining room.
I know the deal. No questions.

Elisabeth Frischauf   13

He never spoke of IT again,
this last conversation with his mother:

*Mother, leave, please. I foresee the city a colossal jail,
you in it.*

My son, dear Vienna will keep me safe.

*Mother, don't fool yourself. Use the visa Karl offers
to go to Australia as his wife.*

Instead, she inscribes two pocket-size volumes of
Goethe's *Faust*:
To my beloved son on his great journey.
Eighteen, he stuffs the books, his Nazi passport
in a small travel bag hoping to disguise his eventual purpose—
first stop, France, to visit a "sick" aunt.
Then, with an affidavit and a ship ticket hidden
under the false bottom of his bag,
to the States.

How long did he beg, use logic while his mother stood fast?
Is this the key? Unpredictable shut down rock, he
explodes, clams shut, mourns without tears

that lap over cheeks,
fall, drop, upon drop, into shirts or sheets,
get lost on sidewalk pavements.

In rage, he mourns.

After each storm he is calm to himself.
Rational, focused, the lawyer–engineer who protects me—
even buying groceries, he's the guy who holds the
door—always.
    Ladies first, he booms in his Viennese-inflected English,
brown eyes a-twinkle, wide, warm grin.

Without him the slightest breeze knocks me over.

LATE HARVEST

1945, the Second World War ends.
Whole lines wiped out: generations, grandmas,
papas, babies . . .
Scattered seeds come on sea winds
Sorrow and sunshine seeds frozen
Vienna seeds lurched by waves to New York shores.

Waiting in my mother
Swimming in my father
new seeds blown, thrown together. New.

One slim volume nests in the bookcase on the long
living room wall,
golden when sunset bathes it—
Verspätete Ernte, Zerstreute Saat (Late Harvest, Scattered Seeds)
Inside, my great-aunt Mitzi's poems wait.

On yellowed pages, they wait for me,
for when I am born, learning English–German–
New York City. Secrets.

Poems Mitzi ploughed and planted, wait for when I can sit,
breathe slow-deep, read, without skipping
the horror glowing inside the prison camp.

Lager Gurs, Juni 1940 (Concentration Camp Gurs)

Die Stimmen verebben jetzt,
Gelächter und Weinen
Von Hunger und Angst gehetzt
Entschlummern die Kleinen,

Voices ebb,
Laughter and sobs
Besieged by hunger and fear
The little ones sleep.

Entschlummern erschöpt die Fraun,
Auf Stroh gebettet,
Und hoffen, dass liebreich ein Traum
Den Kummer glättet

Exhausted women sleep
Bedded on straw`
Hoping that lovingly a dream
Will smooth distress

Mitzi lies with the women in "The black barrack that
whistles with wind. . . ."
in Gurs, southern France—
women herded, shabby, limping
stained, mewling children,
all waiting— for *transport, to "work that makes them free."*

Elisabeth Frischauf   17

Together their stomachs groan for rich butter,
creamy camembert cheese.
Today it's potato skins in watered soup again.
She hungers with them, sows poems
furrow by sleepless furrow.

> Oh, so viel
> Zerschossenes Antlitz
> Und so viel Tote
> So viele Kinder, die allein geblieben . . .

> Oh so many
> bullet-exploded faces
> and so many dead
> so many orphaned children . . .

> Im warmen Bett, in den geschüzten Räumen,
> Kannst du ruhen und träumen?"

> In your warm bed, your protected rooms,
> Can you rest and dream?

The ravening wind spews belated seeds.

Damit nun, doch etwas übrigbleibt/Von alter Liebe
und neuem Leid.
So that something will be left over/from old love and
new suffering.

I, too, sprout songs.

New words.

From Ashes

My refugee parents taught me—*You are your sisters' keeper:*
   Gather cords, frayed, slipping this way–that way,
   between toes, fingers,
   but gather them, bind them together.

Forged from the burnt dead—the great funeral pyre Europe
my stomped, crumpled grandmothers
my mother's hope, scorched crusts.
Countless relatives deleted—
once somewhere, now wisps dangling from the family tree.

My half-breed parents, deemed dirty defilers of the
Aryan race
fled toward the sheer-face cliff.
The kind that keeps rising as they inch upward
shoes torn. No return,
So close to the top.
Years later, my father's need to repeat, *Don't upset your mother!*

Blood-slicked yards, garroted homes in the surrounding
mist, my parents persist.
Raise me along the unknowable way
offer spare hands to strangers

reach within their shrunken pouches
share water and bread.

Luminous, after cold thunder, the rain-comforted world.
Air washed clear. Doves back on the fly.
I am in love with this sudden symphony, a
dream-imbedded vision—
No one dies to make another live:
No one is more, the other less.

Each step my parents showed my small foot where to perch—
left, right, they say, but find the rocky cleft where
through blackened shards, a spiky, yellow dandelion grows.

Dedicated to my parents: Else Pappenheim Frishauf 1911–2009,
Stephen H. Frishauf 1920–2011

First Generation American

Song of earth
song of sky
my people came here.

Song of moon, of wind,
my people came. Refugees
to *Amerika's* liberty.

Holes in their hearts, they had children—
their new start in a new land.
Heartache, with joy, etched fragments.

My people came, admired Yosemite,
praised this hemisphere's bright day—
although it inspired a need for dark glasses in my mother.

Moon and wind song
strange in English
no matter how well we learned it.

Earth and sky magnifies
in vast *Amerika*—So many faces,
lusty bodies twist, twang, and gesture

licking sticky-sugar donuts,
mixing iceberg lettuce with Jell-O.
Not our kind of food!

Each cracked heirloom's shaken song,
dumb weight in the living room.
My people came and were alone.

They did the best they could with torn roots.
Explained patiently German words to my brother,
who impatiently shook them away.

They expected me, first-born, to understand
their tongue the way they did.
I had to learn my in-between way—
here, not there.

Now the grandchildren sing
new song of earth, moon, and sky
today they bring us home.

Around My Heart, A Vise

Beyond their heavy door
the worn blue, living room.
My dream-soaked, yellowed, fifth-grade
fairy doll winks at me from center stage
inside one gray vitrine.

Air thickens.
Echoes from those walls—
Pa's army scream, thunder-green—
    NEVER talk back to your mother!
Ma's black-purple sobs—
    You see, she REALLY doesn't love me.

My legs lock. Bombs go off inside.
I need to retch and heave,
later my guts explode—the runs again.

Burned feelings, shards,
deep frozen in my chest.
There is no murder in my heart, but

my head drums, opens/closes/aches—
Hey, I just arrived, on time—exactly, as Ma insisted.

Every limb, every word my brain can offer, drones
Tired. Oh, so tired.

But my throat opens,
to laugh.
Across the threshold we smile,
    So nice to see you, we gush.
Pa twinkles, Ma bustles.
Brings cinnamon cake and coffee to the table.
We're not so mad after all.

Haunted

Morning about to begin.
I just made love with my husband

In the litter of moments, beautiful and mad
I stare at New York City brick walls.

Coo coo, mourning doves on the window sill:
  Humans are hopeless.

I remember sirens in the streets,
collapsed twin towers
ash-clumped smoke
that sucked into lungs as the wind ran uptown, the day
after 9/11.

Middle-aged, I pace, now that terror is real
America, the haven, doesn't feel safe anymore.

2.

Hitler's smell coats the walls
muffled moans under Grandma Klara's silk *Bokhara*.
Two world wars. Fear and loss stalk my family,

a relentless panther
claws us in our beds,
tucked under thick, downy quilts.

From a gaping hole, blood-laced fur,
his grinning mouth rains baby deer strips
Whirr, wum-wum, his long tail a menacing lasso.

3.

A mother now, with my own two young children
their flushed open faces wait for a cup of cocoa.
    Too hot! Mama.

I blow into the steam—pile on more marshmallows.

Off to your bath now.
Helen is Captain Hook, Jason is Smee,
as they sail the *Jolly Roger* over bubble foam.

Just time to quickly switch on TV news.
A documentary preview flashes:
Nazi Prison Camp Builders—set in verdant Polish spring.

At least Grandma Klara went with her sister.
Were they arm in arm, naked, shivering, shoved
on a surge of others into the poisoned shower?
I vomit. Dash to wash my smeared face.

Elisabeth Frischauf   27

Children, time for bed.
        Mommy, why are your cheeks wet?
        You're jumpy, my daughter says. She feels my distress as
        I lie by them.
It's nothing. Just stubbed my toe.

Later, in my own bed, I battle.
I can't take it anymore. Let me rest!

But the panther purrs and stretches.
Licks fuel off his paws from body-burning ovens.

Compelled to watch, I sit mute.
Must I warm life with ashes?

4.

At midnight I dream:
Whispers from old photos—
Stern, bearded great-grandfather, my plump mother on his lap.
Mysterious ladies in corseted bustle dresses, high-
flung ostrich feather hats.
Great-aunts and grandmas in loose, long-flow shifts.

Rain falls and I become small
climb a bent wire fence. Tear my skirt
skin my knees. Ignore the blood—

I'm leaning over. I want to clear the rain sheet
slicked on the glass wall between me
and those elegant, straight-backed people

but my hands can't keep up.
Rain insists just like when Papa's long legs
made me run to keep up with him.

The panther's green eyes glow.
Perched on the glass wall he growls,

   You are weak, a warped copy of your elders.

Cowed, I croak. Except for my parents
I never knew grandparents, uncles, aunts, cousins . . .
Sssss, a disdainful hiss.
He lopes away.

I shake and wriggle like a wet dog.
Anything to get rid of that pit-sick-in-the-stomach,
roiling hunger for embrace by relatives in my
neighborhood.

5.

Orange dawn.
Outside my window, raindrops glisten in corner shadows.
A carefree dove fluffs her damp feathers.

Elisabeth Frischauf   29

Now that terror is real in America
like a warm cloud, song saunters forth.

I, child of earth, close and balm the wounds.
My hands paint the sky.

I Own Tears for Everyone

Naked, I coil the truth of my existence, scrap upon scrap.
No more childhood rooms where dolls smile
through dark and day.

I stumble. Miss the moon fall
miss the sunrise, the pace of hours.
Chilled dreams. A thick, wet cloth on my face.

    What's wrong with you? Your mother never left
      dishes overnight,
the dishpan scolds.
I wash the dirt down the drain.
That bitter *"don't know"*
drizzles down my throat.

Mama: *Ach,* in her soft, violet-sad-infused voice,
    Hunger hurt so much, I couldn't sleep.
She was four, First World War and twenty years later,
the second. Her life hung.
like a wash line rearranging itself
to make room for the next disaster.

She wanted me to soar
become head physician at Columbia University.

Instead, she clipped my wings:
>   *It is unbecoming for women to be aggressive!*

Mama squeezed tight my lusty, flowing protoplasm. Yet,
she saved herself to give me life
and live as long as she could.

Give me my one moment of delight, I howl.
>   *Did you make your bed?* The pantry shelf leers.
>   *Loser,* the vacuum cleaner snorts, *those dusty piles*
>   *on your desk*
>   *show your mind's a mess.*

My father would take me aside, out of Mama's earshot.
>   *Your mind can go anywhere.*
>   *No one can take it from you.* He advised me,
>   *Become a stewardess!*
>   *Coffee, tea or me. Hah, Hah, hah!*

My face showed him I just saw a grenade explode.
>   *I mean, it's a good way to see the world—*
He tried to make good.

Ouch! GI Joe's toy rifle pierces my heel.
Barbie's svelte torso ridicules my sag.
My children shouldn't have to dry the sinkhole—
children give their breath. They laugh and hold me close.

Please let me be reborn, I bawl to the milk-stocked refrigerator.
A container leaks under the door, a drip so continual
I know, I'll drown.

I own tears for everyone.
My ancestors walked with Einstein, Freud—
I crave Elvis and the Beatles.
I don't stand a chance.

ROOTLINGS

Tears wash the dreamer down the telescope. Where am I?
A chasm climbs over me, thrust upward by a
long-asleep volcano.
Every time I look back, my footsteps erase in ancient sand.
Wo bin ich? I smell warm vanilla-chocolate Guglhupf
(cake). Elves whistle from the pungent pine-forested
rim. I begin to remember in air-English.
German-earth lies down quietly and doesn't complain.

Sun-sky, I awaken. Leave my husband's comfortable embrace.
Last night, his deep round voice, *You're safe!*
broke off my nightmare scream.

Garden Glory, our small patch of land and I, join July.
Cloudless day, ripe for picking sour currant berries.
Crimson juice cruises my American-born palate. Next week
pop-in-the-mouth, sweet gooseberry globes are ready,
with a touch of blood-drop garnish from the bush's thorns.

Tender plot planted by my parents. Transplanted polyglot
Austrian mishmash garden in Putnam County,
New York, USA.

When spring comes, young leaves break
their hard winter husks.
Warm rain and sun flood the soil.
My own roots find their way.

Elisabeth Frischauf 35

Sudden Torrents of Song

Tide swell tongue
up, down toss
breath ebb flow

Moon in the month of my body.

Time flume sea
struggle—all that.
My family, all families

strip, slice, reimagine
relive. Up the voltage.

After all that,
I had to sleep eleven hours.

Sheer sunset
purpled luster
carmine cluster—

All that
from flotsam
sunny surf

Torrents, and I am song

Postscript

NEVER AGAIN!

———⟡———

Shout with me.
Raise your hands, swear
with me and Grosstante Mitzi, my survivor muse,
Never again
ever
NEVER AGAIN!

Part I:

All Over:
They Clasp My Hand

THE CALL

In my garden
tasting a yellow raspberry
smack in the middle of June
the call comes.

You know it will come
yet a slop bucket
sloshes over your head.
And you almost
choke

Your Pa just died.

Grab my purse—leave the lakeside cottage
(the *Landhaus*) —next train to Grand Central
Station—subway to Broadway & 79th—
dash to Riverside Drive & 78th—catch my breath in the
elevator going up

enter my parents' apartment
an orphan. No longer a child.

He is laid out on my mother's side of the bed
where she died, two years ago

unwilling to let go of 98 years,
one week after we celebrate my 64th,
a slice of birthday cake, her last meal.

Pa's wide, strong hands,
freckles faded yellow, veins flat
once rivers of busy use,
folded watchfully on his shrunken chest.

Oh Pa, is all I can say,
soothe his bald, still
slightly warm, domed head.

His caretaker, Telma, makes sure to tell me:
>   *He have his cholcāte ice cream for deener.*
>   *Thees morning he have a beeg bow-el movement. Then he*
>   *lay down and die.*

My brother arrives.

Pa could fix anything until printed circuits. Radios, TVs.
He sharpened his own ax, lawnmower blades—
>   *You name it.*

We sit by the clock on our mother's office desk.
It had developed a habit of running slow—
a problem for timing her psychoanalytic sessions.

We alternate reading aloud
in Pa's long Viennese *ah* for "a,"
Pa's short tale in his notation:
> *1980 +/– . . . an Anachronism in a Synchronous*
> *Motor Drive*

> *The clock . . .was built with ah view to ahssembly*
> *ahnd repair . . .*

> *I opened the housing. Ah small roach was caught on the*
> *main Motor gear!*

> *Careful removal of the remains . . . restored synchronism . . .*
> *Ahnd earned me ah big kiss.*

. *Oh Pa, ever the exacting engineer!*
We laugh
in synchrony
as we part.

A few hours later, I return to rain.
A flower pot sits
In sympathy
on the *Landhaus* doorstep.
Beetle crickets chirp:

Still, still ist Pas Bett (Quiet, quiet Pa's bed)
Füll, füll das Blumenbeet (Fill, fill the flower bed)

I sink Ma's garden trowel, tagged with Pa's red-faded "M"
into damp earth.
Pa's spirit hovers—
grateful hummingbird
heady with fresh lily nectar.

Night falls swift and dark.
Moonlight drowses on the lake beyond
we all love so well.

A firefly brushes my head
where Pa stroked his crying little girl.
My Pa will spend the night in this garden,
he and I love so well.

A candle in the window
lights the night.

By morning Pa is gone.

Grief Swallows

Have you ever seen mist rise into a soft gray sky like fur on
the back of a baby mouse?
Swum in a slate green lake, wash of warm summer rain on
the surface

you a flesh arrow
a clutch of silver bubbles
like grapes when you exhale
into the ripples of your creation?

Swallows dart over me
do their longtail swoops
side to side soar

one swallow, two swallows,
come too-many-to-count-swallows
wind the grief-sky into bulging sheets
I turn my eye, to look;

                  they are gone.

Sky, stock-still, mute
morning off to a slow start
will the sun burn through?

I am left
bereft of all movement
sound.

My father is dead.
A hard man to love.
Tyrannical in his loving
     Make sure you remember your mother's birthday,
he badgered, year after year, all-through her 97th
as if I could forget.

When she died
he became a clock without hands.
I need to see him alive

                         just one more time
no longer obliged to sit silent-still
his same-same joke—
he laughed the hardest—

                         now, one more time, I want to.

Swallow-hollow me
goes about my usual
eat—swim—shower—make bed—
     wake—pay bills—to office—
walk—sit—work—talk—walk—
     sleep—dream—

In the garden morning birds feather sunlight.
Grief swallows wait
asleep in their nest.

A Hard Man to Love

Pa in front, steady at the wheel.

*Up, down. Uh-uhP. No-o-O, down, **DOW-NNN***
in the back seat my brother and I giggle-shout our
made-up game.

Smash, one fist down—his
hits back of child hand—mine
fool-fooling around
collision course
with childhood.
Ours or his?

My hand swells like a football.
Fifty years later the ache finally goes,
but I remember tear-streamed, helpless me.
I skulk, wary in his presence.

Who are you, Pa?

He quotes Goethe, *Faust II*:
> *Wer immer strebend sich bemüht, den können wir erlösen . . .*
> *Whoever strives with all his power, we are allowed to save . . .*
power hat you wore

over your bald domed head
inside maps—
all the rivers of the world

its mountains, its seas.
    You know, the Hudson River begins in Lake Tear in the
    Cloud, high in the
        Adirondacks. The river's really a fjord because it has tides,
Pa trumpets triumphant.

His explorer's gleam that day we're at his desk:
    Ha, ha. Look what I just found.
He opens the small book nestled,
a shaky sparrow in his big hand,
pokes the stuck flyleaf.
Grandmother Klara's striking, clear script dances before us:
    Diesen Faust hast du dir gewünscht, mein geliebter Sohn.
    Hab immer so schöne wünsche und mögen sie alle in
    Erfülling gehn!
        Mutter—Dienstag, Wien 10. Januar 1939

Years later he translates in his memoirs:
    To my beloved son, you wished for this Faust.
    Always have wishes, which are so beautiful and may they
    all be fulfilled!
        Mother—Tuesday, Vienna, January 10, 1939

Elisabeth Frischauf   49

Now he fusses with the split cover
and a cruise brochure on his desk—one he'll never take
won't look at me, the mist in my eyes

What does a mother say to her only beloved child she
knows she will never see again?

1943 she is murdered in Auschwitz.

Minutes drag.
I stand by him at attention.
My feet have learned to count
won't dare interrupt
lulled into lapping silence: Must not provoke a cataclysm!

Isn't there a better use for our time?

Save Everything

Time to close up forty years of my parents' life in
this apartment.

Soon, no more visits
no more time to waver—
blue crystal bowl or tulip-neck floor vase?

Footsteps clap where
thread-worn carpet lay.

Corners, cabinets
shelves, shoeboxes,
drawers bulge:
>*You might need it someday.*

Gift labels, light bulbs, birthday cards, shopping bags:
>*You name it.*

I plunge into Pa's study.
Thick walnut wood floor-to-ceiling bookcases.
Typewriter table modified for an old Apple computer—
that sloped, blue plastic bubble around a screen.

Handy pile of scrap paper for printing emails. Each one
hand stamped
sent/received, with date. Computer, mouse, email made a
late entrance.

A long Danish teak two-level desk commands the
room's center.
Two lovers in a swing and a glass porcupine frolic on top.
Epoxy's extravagant shine betrays the repaired middle
drawer handle crumbled from wear.

Hard to grab, I fumble, teeter on a knife edge.
What will I find?

His photo, must be sixteen,
catches my eye
strapping, six-foot tall, open-faced guy.

I know he was strong.
Five years old, hauled coal buckets up five flights,
swam, hiked, or skied every weekend
bicycled old crooked streets all over Vienna,
which he never forgot.

US Army dog tags rest in a field
of stapler refills, paper clips,
their border marked by his prized
plastic slide rule.

Deep in the drawer's corner, a Japanese lacquer box,
two lucky cranes streaking over a full moon on its
clamped cover.
Inside, crushed by random bunches of keys
a torn-off envelope return label.

My face flares hot. Damn!
My hidden guilt—
I know this was his last lover.

I was raw, still in love with my ex-husband
who sported a new woman twinkling over him
while I was buried in night duty during pediatric internship.

> *Stop wailing about your ex. Waste of time. Get up, study,*
> *make sure you eat.*
> *You have a valuable medical degree to support you. Meet*
> *me and we'll ski together,* Pa writes to me in a postcard
> from his business combined
with skiing trip to Tirol.

He believes in shock treatment.

Yes, Pa, I mumble to myself.
I'll join you to *schuss* away my wounds,
meet you and your Austrian business clients.
Get to know you?

There **she** is. Marianne.
I see Pa leap, glide
a hoppy teenage hare
free from Ma's care.

How could I ever tell Ma I knew,
even when she eventually found
Marianne's love letter open on the foyer table?

Delve Deeper

Under that lacquer box
a fat black swastika.
Pa's German passport cover
he never showed me.

I start to piece the puzzle.
March 12, 1938
Leg up—straight blade
        Arm up—Arrow-shaft right arm
              Sieg, Sieg
                   Heil

Hitler swarms Austria.

March 13, Pa walks the Albertgasse to his Technical
High School.
Der Führer's portrait blazes
over twisted black crosses
a new teacher shoves Pa:
    There! Your classroom for Jews and Mischlings (half -Jews).

Pa is now *dirty*
a target for toughs
to curse and beat him,
police cheering them on.

Day by day Nazi racial laws
clobber Germany's acquired *Volk*.

I meet Pa's aunt Laura, his mother's youngest sister,
for the first time on a page in his memoirs,
drowning in a folder sunk in a stuffed file drawer.

She was scraping by as a French teacher in a secretarial school.
A Jewess.
Dismissed.

She is the one who taught Pa French so he could impress
clients later on:
>   *Can you test if this rope on the safety belt will hold me?*
>   *I might as well clean the windows,* she asks Pa, the family
handyman/engineer-to-be.

Laura hangs herself.

>   *Her neck was so long. Don't go see her corpse,*
>   *before she's cremated,* Klara, his mother, tells him.
Can one ever forget?
Pa writes 70 years later.

Klara, his mother, respected, valued
insurance claims officer
for the huge Mannheimer Versicherungsgesellschaft,

another Jewess
forced
to retire.

Every morning, each afternoon,
Pa with teenage blowtorch intensity
tries to melt her marble resolve
against a friend's visa offer to save her.

> *I cannot leave my last remaining sister and besides,*
> *my pension comes in.*

It does.
That pension, like a monthly IV drip to death,
continues up through their deportation to Auschwitz in 1943.

Lamplight over the kitchen table.
Hastily brushed away ham roll dinner crumbs.
Pa sits next to his mother writing letters. *Urgent!*
to distant relatives in Chicago.
Pa will leave
as soon as they can sponsor a US visa.
Across the city, in their apartment, Mitzi and Hermann
mash two leather
armchairs together. Horsehair's snapped strands of
stuffing pierce
the thick split seams. The shaky legs barely manage to lean
on each other.

Married in 1918, Mitzi is Ma's aunt (her father's younger
sister) and
Hermann, Pa's uncle (the older brother of his father)

Looking long into each other's sunken eyes,
>*Let's divorce.* Unusual for Mitzi, she fumbles for words.
>*Communist-Jew, I'm a grave danger to you. Join me in Paris.*
>*Soon. As a dermatologist, I can earn enough there. The Nazis*
>*won't bother you, a non-political Aryan.*

Hermann *is* arrested as a communist.
Sent to Buchenwald to do forced labor.
In 1942, cachectic and deathly ill with TB
he is exonerated and released to die alone.

Hermann, Pa's father figure—
Pa is one year old when his father Walter divorces his mother,
leaves Vienna behind to live with his aging mother in Graz.
When Pa turns six he meets his father again with only brief
summer visits thereafter.
Walter will voluntarily join the Nazi Party.

Even so, Pa, his only child, sends him a goodbye letter
(never acknowledged) but, only after
Pa is safely on his way to the USA.

Before his death in 1953, Walter, in his will disowns Pa:
>*My putative son of the Jewess Klara.*

Events speed up decisions in every branch of Pa's family.
Pa's uncle Erich (father Walter and Uncle Hermann's
oldest brother)
with his daughter, Erika,
experienced mountaineers, hike one weekend,
(late 1939/1940)
on the Rax mountain's limestone crag.

Fall

into eternity.

I reach way, way back,
into the farthest corner of Pa's drawer, I find real ashes. Ma's
in the original mailing carton from 2009,
after she died, almost 98, at home.

I cannot tell you how my brother and I decide
I take her.

REVENGE

Pa, 18, will use that swastika passport.
Goodbye to *Mutter*, goodbye *liebchen* Tully,
his puppy love, goodbye friends all trying to leave
for Turkey, Shanghai, Czechoslovakia, Bulgaria . . .

Train to Aunt Mitzi, who believes
she is untouchable
in Paris.

Goodbye Europa.

Late winter 1939, visa, ship's trunk, skis—edges sharp, shined
by engineer Uncle Erich,
Pa boards the Cunard line to New York.

A few days later, his last dollars for the ticket,
he rides the Greyhound bus to Chicago.
His stranger relatives hug him for the first time.

Pa, elevator boy
Christmas package wrapper,
studies during work breaks.
Any job to supplement his meager stipend.
Three years later he graduates, the electrical engineer at last!

Sunday, December 7, 1941
    A date which will live in infamy . . . sharp rise in his voice,
Pa eagerly quotes FDR.

Pearl Harbor blasted.
The US declares war on Germany and Japan.
December 8, Pa is an enemy alien.

He tries to enlist:
    No. Wait until they draft you, he's told.
He waits with a job in New York, designing
the Pennsylvania Railroad's overhead electric line system,
used for decades.

August 1942, turns 22. September, the US Army calls him up.
He becomes an American citizen
anglicizes his given name.
Casts out the "c" from his family name, Frischauf.
Now Frishauf, he separates himself from what's left
on the other side of the Atlantic.

I will put back the cast out "c" into my family name.
So the books I write could stand with
Great-Aunt Mitzi's.

A corporal in the US Army Signal Corps Pacific Theater
victorious with his new country, Pa musters out in Seattle.

He dials the phone to my yet-to-be mother in New York City:
May I stay with you, while I get my bearings?

They know each other from childhood.
Plus the link: Mitzi, married to Hermann.

Passion sparks. In 1946 they marry and ground their
New World family.
With me, born in 1947, and two years later, my brother.

In 1957, Pa will successfully challenge his father's hurtful will.
Postwar Austria, has reinstated its ancient law:
A father cannot disinherit his son.

Two Renaissance portraits:
a Dutch schoolmaster and St. John the Baptist
follow the court's decision in Pa's favor to New York.

Clear-eyed, forward looking, they
glance at the Hudson River
instead of his father's dark Graz shade.

My brother and I each take one
as we empty our dead parents' apartment.
Our only pieces of this enigma-grandfather.

On a regular Sunday visit sitting with Pa in his study,
shortly before he died in 2011, a sudden moment
of bonhomie:
>   *I saw a thing or two, fighting the Japanese in New*
>   *Guinea.* Silence.

He swiveled in his worn maroon chair and surfed over
that dread,
dropped pause:
>   *But then, I felt good selling my GI cigarettes and chocolate*
>   *to hungry Japs on the black market in Osaka.*
>   *And whenever I could,*
>   *I gave extra* (probably 1945, after the Japanese surrender).

He pointed toward the bedroom wall. There, since they
married, over their bed
hung the red silk, gold-embroidered Buddhist altar cloth.
A trade he made
with a bent-over, wan widow. Her family treasure, for food.
>   *Turn your back, look forward. Don't dwell, like your*
>   *mother,* he finishes.

Did he shoot between two eyes flashing through the dense,
dim jungle green
to save himself? Wriggling on the humid ground, did he
hear groans,

glimpse the twisted, writhing body? Ants and worms
feasting on mounds of dead?

That pause,

plunged into my core. Dragged deep, that ordinary day,

I forgot to come up for air.

Up the Ladder

Okay, Pa, here we go.
Let me tackle your bookshelves
my ski legs
rung by rung
to the tippy-top—
up there nine feet
in your study
an aluminum pie plate
you shoved above the fixture.
Now shadows sashay zigzag
between the slits you cut.

I hear your voice:
> *Scatters light, saves electricity. You might need it someday.*

Yes! In the darkest corner I see your favorite author's
complete works
spot on:
> *Nothing shows a man's character more than what he
> laughs at,* Goethe,

a crumbled mess.
Down it drops
fierce dust cloud
into a black garbage bag.

DOORS OPEN. DOORS CLOSE.

Have you ever listened to the sound of a hollow, a solid
wood door?
Wondered, do they open to the underworld or the palm
of heaven?

Thunk. Door opens.
PuMM, closes.
Acoustic tile seals
what is said inside.

In true Viennese fashion, Ma's medical office/study
is a sequestered room in this sprawling apartment.

Her Underwood in the corner, would jam
two m's together, levitate capital "W" above the line of text.

Under the window, dark blue wool-weave psychoanalytic
couch.
A low bookshelf discretely hides her dove-gray listening chair.

On a small table opposite, rotary phone,
notepad, appointment book, alabaster globe lamp
like the full moon
inside this quiet room.

Crisscross the hallway, waiting room, patient's bathroom
I shared growing up,
reconstruct Ma's 86th street office before this one—
and where my childhood bedroom was
until I left home, 20 years old.

Weekday pulse:
clap clap patients' leather soles
on foyer linoleum. *Tuhp tuhp*
Ma's low heels.
Doors open. Doors close.

Ka Pla-ap—oak-wood door shuts.
Ma's in there with a stranger.
I am shut out, six years old.

What does a stranger talk about to Ma—lying down?

Do they have bad dreams like me?
Night after night, asleep in my warm bed, I hear
Smash, cra-sh-Rr-eek black boot men-big
splinter the solid door, *stomp stomp*

through the monster hole.
I must not squeak, sneeze, burp under my bed
or they will find me. Gestapo.

Elisabeth Frischauf   67

I've heard Ma and Pa whisper the word
and scraps of stories. That sudden door knock, forced entry—
that was Vienna, but they could come to 86th Street too.
I scrunch chest to head. Am I small enough?

One afternoon, I'm probably nine,
ear on her office door, I listen—
Ma's voice too soft.
The stranger murmurs.

Maybe they are both asleep?
Bewildered, I wait in the kitchen, until
Swush, hooray! the door swings Ma in for her break

blue haze of cigarette, my itchy nose
doesn't stop her long pull-puff
black coffee sip with aluminum thermos ring shine.
For ten minutes, I get her silver voice:
   The patient leaves worries on the couch.

Later, when Ma is out shopping, I try it.
Talk to heavy books on her shelves.
R-R-uhgh the 86th street crosstown bus
groans up the rise below.

Even though the Nazi boots vanish, they come back like
Ma's patients.

B-zzz, br-r-ing, Sla-agh the metal
front door sucks the next patient in
Hall-oh, Ma says.
I am on my own. But, I've forgotten to ask her why
nightmares don't dissolve.

Two mothers: Ma and Medical Doctor-Ma.
Keen neurologist, psychoanalyst, kind teacher
to me, psychiatrist yet-to-be in the kitchen,
to her medical residents at the teaching hospital.

We listen, learn:
> *Like all people, some patients are nice and others not so nice.*

> *Because a patient is psychotic does not mean he or she is
> immoral and will kill or steal.*

When I am a graduated psychiatrist and try to share
my knowledge—
family therapy (a mainly American idea), new medications,
she remains in Vienna
with her many Nobel Prize-winning professors,
venerated Professor Tandler who drew the human body
with both hands at once.
> *Not so much went wrong in life for you,* she flings
the long bone of her finger that holds
war goodbyes, too wrenching to count.

How could my recently arrived mother in 1938,
be prepared that America's
justice–freedom promise excluded "colored people"
and the continuation
of menacing, whispered discrimination against Jews?

American girl at Ma's feet
I lose her, lose me
learn to scramble in gray's
quick slam over light
where I see you, **You** don't see me.

I never could work up to my baby's
delivery like you. I stand in your shadow.

Never will I become your daughter–colleague
like **You** in letters with your father,
Grandpa Martin.

How doors can fly open and we disconnect.

Baltimore

Early morning pink flush on wintry strips of gray,
shaky Amtrak clacks
along the northbound tracks. Empty windows stare back,
broken, slaggard, no use no more—
Baltimore.

Hooh ee haagh the triton whistle (devil's interval)
hacks my reverie.
No sweep of peace
no major soothe of *da da dee, da da da* (a Beethoven divine
sixth melody)
on this stretch of track.

1938, my yet-to-be mother steps unsure, off the
Nieuw Amsterdam.
Years later, she remembers a firm New York City pier
two bright hustle-bustle days, before going off to her job,
the guarantee behind her rescue.

No slate-gray, slim-suited
SS boys sit across from her now
discussing how you spot Jews
by their noses. To beat up or kill.

Seven hours later, the snub-nosed Greyhound lumbers
into slum-girdled
downtown Baltimore, *too dangerous at night.*
She finds a cheap hotel.

5 a.m., dark December.
Black-bold sea trunk snaps open to her trembling key.
What to wear on this first day?

Her breath darts.
Like a worried sparrow, she must pick sense
through word swarms
quick and dense.

I see her creased gray-blue eyes—It will be the wing
sleeve, high-neck, fawn rayon dress,
chestnut sash, tied into a perky bow,
low-heeled coffee-brown oxfords.

Over it all, starched white coat, royal blue Johns Hopkins logo
and her name, embroidered on the small breast pocket.
It crackles while she bends,
sends a sharp reflection
in the "White Only" drinking fountain.

Her soft Viennese-inflected English
must learn Jim Crow—

in the waiting room of the elegant Phipps Clinic,
coat hangers neatly labeled, "White" and "Colored,"
at the decrepit, rat-infested Spring Grove State Hospital.

I see its brick buildings through the train's streaked window
atop a slope lovely, smooth and grassy.
My yet-to-be mother wrenched from imperial boulevards,
ward psychiatrist for mad colored women.

Her days off, she explores the *better* neighborhoods, their
country clubs (Jews excluded).

Unwilling wanderer, she had to leave her *Mutti* behind
in Nazi Vienna, go
say farewell to her *Papa* in Tel Aviv
retrieve her US visa and affidavit in Jerusalem, sail to Trieste
then the train to Marseilles, then Paris, where it's farewell
Tante Mitzi.

Finally the train to Boulogne-sur-Mer.
Up the narrow gangway onto the double-stacked cruise liner,
still polished from her maiden voyage a few months earlier,
filling up with more Hitler refugees, in Cherbourg,
Southampton.

Scattered between the exiles,
a few wealthy Americans as yet untouched by war
returning from the Grand Tour.

Europe cuts away.
My yet-to-be mother is alone
crossing to the unknown
to Baltimore.

Sorting Fragments

Moonlight's dazzle stutters.
Shine transmutes dawn's waiting
to sunshaft soliloquy
that lights Ma's life-lantern
once again.

Screaming in her brain, raining confusion
slipshod bits of her past paste
scrambled words with labored breath.

I've become her *Mutti* and she mutters:
   Es ist egal wo ich bin (*it doesn't matter where I am*)
and swallows. I sense she wants to keep this to herself.

   Bussi, bussi, Kiss, kiss, Pa pleads.
Reflexively she puckers her lips—
powerless to resist.

Ma soldiers on. Confides to me and my daughter—
treasured granddaughter: *He needs me. He is not ready to be alone.*

   Laugh, come give me a laugh, Pa implores.
She gropes in the lurch
of a transient ischemic attack.

Laugh she cannot find.

> *Professor Durig. Erinnerung an unsere Reise nach Voralberg.*
> *(Professor Durig. Remember our trip to Voralberg),* she slurs.

1936 mist she clings to
and 1956 when we all visited him.
Our first trip "Home" to Austria.

The mist lifts as suddenly as it fell.
She is back to us.

Always modest, she picks at her dress,
pulls it up, exposes herself.
I came out from there, her first baby.

It seems impossible from her shrinking body,
but Ma did the impossible.
Nine times like a cat when
we thought she was dying—
I know I came through iron.

Why don't you die already,
spare us this *yo-yo* time? (My mind reflexively wants out)

Love hushes corners
crooks its charming finger: *Follow, follow, tracks into the*
gleaming unknown!

A dash of fear sweeps along the edges
like foam cups a sea wave,
froths and bursts from tension.

    It is the wave that carried wiry Eleazar, Ma whispers.
    He is mine. I take his soul. Ganz still, ganz schön
    und wunderbar
    (All quiet, all beautiful and wonderful.)

I don't understand, but realize
Ma's body will not be taken.
Not for now.

WHEN MA DIES

Her Lanz heart-strewn nightgown
billows as she thrashes and pants acetone breath.
Her breath rasps empty gums.

Dim January afternoon, I lie next to her.
Toothless baby-faced photos grin from the bedroom walls
mine, my brother, her grandchildren.

Kuck kuck, the cuckoo clocks out
our remaining hours. Pa is next door.
Laboring over taxes.

Oh my *Mütterchen,* you had such hope.
Wordless, you held my hand yesterday—
our last knowing.

Not today. I speak to her restless body:
 Liebe Mama, ruh dich aus. Du kannst uns verlassen.
 Du warst so lang mit uns; hast so gekämpft. (Dear Mama, rest.
  You can leave us. You were with us so long; fought so.)

Please live, I wish.
But she dies.

Lap-lapping wait time gone
watch-time done.

We share this terrible wrench like birth.
A tear travels down my nose
like raindrop tremble on leaf's edge.
I do not allow it to fall.

Come back.
Protect me, I cry.

You could not imagine
the harm you could do—
others' needs first, then yours
and lastly mine.

You could not imagine how
the rimless seam of loss-past would haunt me.

You will never know who I am or what I become.

I seal myself inside Ma's office. She is mine again.
No oceans to cross, our cells hum.

Womb-time
before questions never asked, never answered.

Elisabeth Frischauf　79

We are one sea. No one else can claim or take you.
Come back.

Let us translate our itinerary into words.

Pa's Cancer

The loudest cry Pa can muster:
>   *I need you!*
pierces the soundproof office door.
I open it.

Up to now, Pa refuses help.
My attempts inconvenient, *weak womanliness.*

How strong Pa was. Again and again his long arm drove
the pickaxe,
Pung, cruck, the clay hard-pan yields at our *Landhaus.*
Clu-ung. Rock strike.
>   *Putnam County potatoes,* he jokes.
Swings his sledge hammer. *Smash.*

He wouldn't interrupt dictation of complex patent applications,
in English,
German, or French, while we waited,
stomachs growling
smell of pot roast
going cold.
>   *I wasn't long. Nothing critical is happening,*
>   he'd sputter loudly.

Ma and I, *the female of the species*,
know he feels in command.
We've heard him say over and over: *Because I say so!*

Cancer now controls Pa.
Terror's green-bile gleam stares.
No-hiding
no-more.

Under his hollow, unsteady voice: *Nothing hurts,*
a whiff of mushroom decay.

His muscular mind encased
like *Epoxy* he cheerfully slathered
over cracks. At first a flexible goop,
that you think you can still shape or tear, but no.
It's bonded into rock-shell.

We walk slow to the kitchen nook.
He eats half a cookie.
Needs a nap he never used to.

Ma's Secrets

Like an aircraft carrier, a broad five-foot wide, steel-case
desk oversees her office.

Its many drawers filled. Prescription pads,
business cards, stethoscope, reflex hammer.

In the locked drawer, bank books, household cash,
old brown-bottled, rarely handed-out drug samples:
Quaaludes, Valium, Dexedrine—years ago liberally supplied.

Pa followed her strict order:
   Stay out of my desk!
which he kept until she died.

When I begin to use this office
to see *my* patients
and keep an eye on him.

   Don't change anything, he insists.

My patients sit in an oversized swivel chair,
shaped like a comforting hand.
I use the analytic couch to rest between my sessions.

New samples: Prozac, Zoloft, Lexapro, Lamictal line
the drawer
where I find the note
Pa never did
about the piano.

Under the tray of paper clips
under the 2001 Audubon calendar
the handwritten note
her mashed letter German script:
> *Ich vermiss das Klavier, wie einen Menschen . . .*
> *Es tut weh. Das Einzige aus der Vergangenheit,*
> *aus der Kindheit. (I miss the piano like a person . . . It hurts.*
> *The only thing from the past, from childhood.)*

One day this piano vanishes.
Pa donates it to my brother's high school alma mater.

How her long slim fingers caressed the svelte, honey-wood
Steinway Grand.
Beethoven's *Für Elise* flumed corners
Brahms *Wiegenlied* hushed the ceiling
Schumann's *Carnaval* dashed across the floor.

Until she went blind
eight years before she died.

Under the blue blanket she crocheted,
the Steinway stared at us,
like a jilted cow ruminating her cud
every Sunday dinner.

My heart drops its beat
as if a hornet jabbed straight in.
Ma-ma is music.

Light fingertips cajole tight strings.
We sing—my brother and me in her lap
sunk back, almost inside her womb.

Oh Donau so blau (Oh Danube so blue)
the edelweiss-embroidered strap waltzes
with the guitar, she bought with her first savings
at a Baltimore pawnshop.
Swing Low, Sweet Chariot
the Hudson River begins to rock.

Trois Jeunes Tambours (Three Young Drummers),
we march,
jaunty, defiant conquerors.

Ma-ma is music.

Sunday Dinner

From the apartment's den: *Clang, clash, chunk.*
My brother unloads Pa's workbench
bowed, splintered—years of saw blade, hammer blow.

Together we dismantle the teak dining table.
R-Ruck it sighs, gives up its warped expander leaves—
forty years
of family dinner. Every Sunday.

If we made excuses to miss:
 All right, don't come, (but eat guilt for supper.)

Serviettenknödl-steamed dumpling
would emerge, slung on a cloth napkin
suspended within my parents' pressure cooker:
 Much more practical than that fancy nightgown
 we got as a wedding gift! they'd giggle.

Next heaps of red cabbage and salad.
 Prosit, cheers!
We raise green-footed Austrian wine glasses
swallow any disagreement
beneath fruity *Grüner Veltliner*

special import from the store on Manhattan's
West 72nd street
once a cheap neighborhood
where German speaking refugees used to
meet at Café Éclair, their *ersatz* Vienna or Berlin.

So much depended on what you could afford.

1956, Our First Trip Home

From Idlewild airport—our take-off whirs through
red-and-white-cloth-curtained
windows—my brother and I visit the pilot's cabin—
glowing knobs, winking dials,
green and red indicator dots—we sit on his lap—inside
a bowl of stars.

Early 1900s Vienna-style apartment building on
the Arndtstrasse,
up four winding flights of marble stairs,
expectant heavy wood double door
claps open like a giant clam.

Is this what it feels like to be hugged by an octopus?
In New York it's only four of us.
    Servus, Hallo, Hehlo

Great-Aunt Mitzi, her son, Hans, Helene, his wife,
their children: Annemarie, nine like me,
Heinrich, seven just like my brother,
and Frau Jesczek, loyal nanny/housekeeper
surround us.

Long-leg Pa, longer-legs Hans, the two
boys, same side-to-side-swing walk.
Ma, Great-Aunt Mitzi, we girls, that same
super-bony bump on our wrists.

The grown-ups lapse into Viennese.
Hoppsa, hooray, we four kids race
Fast dizzy-faster loops around the eight-foot mahogany table,
off duty now—
later, Helene's family practice patients
will sit here, wait, chat, knit.

Click-click Frau Jesczek's knees creak time
with her complaints. She makes sure we hear
her huff carrying heavy trays loaded with
Wienerschnitzel, cucumber and potato salad,
traditional 12–2 o'clock main meal of the day.

We understand her drill sergeant finger point.
Slide into stiff high-backed chairs, giggle
barely reach the scored, shiny tabletop
bang our feet into each other, whoop

and settle to sip fresh alpine milk
through strawberry and chocolate flavor straws,
chemical postwar magic we've brought.

Elisabeth Frischauf   89

Welcome gifts we'll keep sending with clothes,
cigarettes, peanut butter
every month.

Sunday, we play hide and seek in the Vienna Woods,
climb to the Cobenzl Terrace Restaurant,
stuff ourselves like other Viennese families
with strudel drenched in vanilla sauce.

Pa and Ma beam. Point over the woods, the vineyards:
    Look, down there the Stephansdom, the city's heart.
    No building can be higher than its spire.

Ma's cheeks glisten. Pa grins big ear to big ear.
We squint to find their neighborhoods,
the medical university, the giant Ferris wheel
in the Prater Park, where we'll go next.

Every day Ma's steady smile
Pa's feet on wings.
We're on a magic carpet
through streets they remember so well.

Bomb-scarred buildings, blurred dots in our peripheral vision.
The grim past temporarily banished.

The tour guide in Schönbrunn Palace marches everyone
to the next room.
1-2-3, I waltz. The ballroom's high gilt-framed mirror
reflects my rose-draped crinoline, so stiff I can whirl
on my side!

My seven-year-old brother chases, eats.
Nine-year-old, I can be a princess in a real palace!

Where were you? I'm bored, my brother hisses, when I catch up.

1-2-3 he's all smiles. Hazelnut ice cream,
his new favorite, streaks
his cheeks as we end our tour at the café.

We can't get enough.

Too soon the trip to our Austrian homeland is over.

Elisabeth Frischauf   91

The Chandelier

Piece by piece this four-foot-long palace chandelier
follows us by ship in a wooden crate
home to New York City.

Commanding empress, she hangs centered over my
parents' dining table,
miraculous survivor of multiple wars
handed down the female line
for five generations.

Pa slowly turns up the dimmer switch.
New electric candles, his handiwork, spread light.
I, my brother, our spouses
and children prefer a brighter room,
yet the chandelier dazzles.

Hundreds of crystal prisms spray us,
the shuttered walls—blaze blue,
pink, phosphor green, orange gold.
We, the New World half of family, sit
shimmered in Vienna's orbit.

Pa repeats his jokes
Ma slides her soft a's underneath.

Soon they spark over each other
joust in accented English
    thrust
        back/forth,
            in/out
                *Side with **me**,* they each demand
as they round the rainbow *champs de guerre.*

    Pow, Pow, my four-year-old son points his gun-shaped
thumb and index finger.

    God damn it! Pa slams his fist onto the table. *Don't
ever do that!*

We freeze. My frightened son looks away.
A tinkerer like Pa, they will never bond.
    All you're really interested in is the goddamn computer,
Pa would accuse him.

To everyone's surprise, the computer bypassed Pa,
once the forward-looking engineer.

The chandelier's magic could not hold us.
Stiff backs, necks, we next generations make brief stabs
to be heard,
activate the failsafe switch: *Food's getting cold!*
Raise forks, knives, chew.

Elisabeth Frischauf   93

Darkling at our feet, the unquenchable sluice of loss, pools.

Ring after ring, my brother and I now pack
the chandelier's glittering glass.
Its airy bronze candle-bearing orb
we carry, surprised by its weight,
to my waiting station wagon.

Ma's Slim Black-Lacquered Bookcases

Floor to ceiling, on two opposing walls, forlorn shelves beg
for attention.

We are from the time of books.

Can you imagine opening a dusty, tattered leather-bound
book from 1771?
Paper made from rags, still firm, straight, and supple.
On the flyleaf,
my maternal great-great-grandfather sent his fountain
pen skating
his signature in barely legible script!

The printed pages he held, clear and sharp
in classic German Gothic type.
If I squint I see the "s" is not an "f"
because there is no tiny line
pushing out of its stem.

Another shelf has medical reprints from papers Ma wrote—
some in German, many in English. Worldwide
correspondence surrounds them.

Older books flash gilt bindings between flat
modern paperbacks.
Her favorite authors: Mörike, Ebner Eschenbach,
Stifter, Canetti, Dreiser, Pearl Buck, and
four leather-bound volumes of Dickens's *Bleak House.*

Enveloped by Volume II, reading to perfect her English
before landing
in New York Harbor, two SS boys enter her train
compartment in
Bad Reichenhall where she went to say goodbye to her aunts.

They jabber eagerly:
   Easy to spot a Jew. That big hook of a nose.
They do not notice hers plunge,
her flush, her quickened breath.
   They assumed I'm British, she told us.

Does every single book here have a story?

The Search for Early Man drops from a high shelf.
Where is early woman?
Lost within the covers?
Do we usually disappear so readily?

Ma, come back.
I can talk to you now
and I believe you will listen.

THE LETTERS

We are from the time of postcards and letters.
Bundles, sheaved with broken, gooey rubber bands.

On the bottom bookcase shelf, boxes and boxes.
Split, valiant containers of too much,
labeled Mutti, Papa, Miscellaneous

Dust-sore, my eyes, for the first time see
Ma's early secret life—

> drowsy Bad Reichenhall summers
> where Aunt Lottie fed her cream puffs
> teatime scene behind lace-hushed curtains—cascading
> collapse of their world outside the window frame.

> Eighteenth birthday yet to come, exuberant blue-tone
> postcards to Leo, Fritz, Harry—lovers?

Written before Jews Do Not Belong buried them.

Mutti's Letters

Have you ever held tissue-thin pages that tremble with
your breath?
That float as you turn them over?

A riot of rose blooms collaged on a plastic binder cover
conceal three years of letters between Ma
and Mutti (my grandmother Edith) who could not leave—
her quota number too high. She must return
to her birth country, Germany, and
her brother-in-law and sister's house—
three trapped Jews.

Edith waits. Hopes, waits for that visa,
that affidavit to bring her safe
to her daughter in America.

Twist/turn, yes/no, it's coming, but
the Nazis want more money.
Ma has the affidavit, borrows money for the ship's ticket,
but the German exit visa clearing office closes for months.
Mail delivery to Jews cut.

Swallowed tears fleck the room.
I strain to see nothing

beyond that swollen purple space
round my eyes.

Each letter from Edith says:
> *Du wirst sehen, es wird noch alles gut und schön für uns.*
> *(You will see, all will turn out good and beautiful for us.)*

Ma's birthday, May 22, 1941, Edith writes:
> *Das Kleeblatt fand ich an deinem Geburtstag.*
> *Warten und hoffen wir.*
> *(I found the clover leaf on your birthday.*
> *We'll wait and hope.)*

Each letter pales.
Distance stretches.
Edith hunted—
the game always changes.
She'll need luck
lots of it
to escape.

Letter from her ex-husband, Ma's father Martin,
suggests Edith
fully embrace Judaism, (in Nazi Germany!) and immigrate
to Palestine,
where she can temporarily live with him and his third wife.

April 1943, letter addressed: Spring Grove Hospital, Maryland,
where Ma is staff psychiatrist:

> *Rather than be taken to a concentration camp, your mother*
> *took Veronal with her sister and brother-in-law. She sank*
> *into peace, your photograph on her lap.*

I hear my mother's strangled voice:

> *I could never raise enough money to rescue my mother.*
> *She wasn't Jewish enough, as a Protestant half Jew,*
> *for the US Hebrew agencies to help, and then it was too late.*

Ma is in the midst of studies that year
to establish her US medical credentials.
She has to learn of her mother's death
months later from a letter with its own story—smuggled
to a family friend escaped to Switzerland.

Then her father's death in Tel Aviv,
from an obituary in the *New York Times*.

Alone
in this alien, fecund land
except for memories.

Holes

Rain and bells bang bones.
Grave holes brim poppies.

Forget-me-nots
          vie for attention.

Know/don't know holes shrink
and grow, inconstant
               except

as companions
to a child of refugees
                  where holes are to hide in.

ANY OTHER DAY

To greet the day is a delicate matter.
After walking manic moonsteps,
is love more free to roam at night?
Is swimming easier by moonlight?

Thick with dreams
coated by sweet urgency,
how long is never
again
at 64? At 67?

Later?

When the low-lally
Aufwiedersehen, goodbye
finished.

Wiedergutmachen (Reparations)
the name of today's game—
in Austria, in Germany.

Understand?
Remind?

Then leave it.

Lose it?

An "other" day begins.

Ma's sorrow my breakfast.
Pa's rage for dinner.
I tried to swallow the pain,
baked into their words, hands, eyes.

My growing up, mother-myself years
chunks sad and lonely
kept me glued
in the yawing pit with them.
Too afraid I'd lose them
if I walked away.

Klara and Edith's Letters

Klara (Pa's mother) and Edith (Ma's mother) corresponded?
I did not know they were friends!
Two lost mothers, stripped—
their only children gone
to America.

Now I understand the lock clamping my parents together.
Exile, their Viennese German—
an at-home language for each other,
their only mothers
forced by Hitler and his followers' hatred
to die.

Papa's Letters

introduce me to Martin, Ma's father.
Details behind the bespectacled, furrow-
lined face in a black-and-white photograph
on Ma's dressing table.

1933. Martin leaves Vienna for Palestine,
promised the Department
of Neurology Chairmanship at Tel Aviv's new
medical school.

Refused (no details here), bitter,
about to return to Vienna,
his sister, Great-Aunt Mitzi warns:
    Do not come back. You, a socialist, will be arrested.
The Austro-fascists are in power since he left.

He stays. Builds a successful psychiatry and neurology practice.
I find a fat plastic mailer envelope with hundreds of his 1937
letters in English:
    Esteemed colleagues: . . .
in Sweden, Switzerland,
Iowa, Chicago, Baltimore.

My daughter, Assistant in the Neurology–Psychiatry clinic
at the University of Vienna, was dismissed under Nazi racial
laws. She urgently needs a job to leave for safety.

Answer follows answer from well-placed physicians:
    I wish I could, but . . .
until Dr. Adolf Meyer, says *YES* and
gives her an unpaid position
at the Johns Hopkins Phipps Clinic in Baltimore.

She will live!

Miscellaneous Letters

Did you know that paper has its own memory? Refolded,
it rebels,
cracks, splits. Ink leak, tear splotch, blood, held tight
within the fibers.

1983–1987 letters between Ma and her best friend
Marie Langer
through their avant-garde high school, medical school,
psychoanalytic studies—

written after they found each other again
two white-haired ladies with grandchildren,
beginning to believe in patches of lives
well spent—Ma in New York City, Marie in Mexico.

Forty years apart. In danger, fleeing.
Future uncertain. Loved family members, friends
murdered, suicided,
these two tough women
made new lives out of ashes.

How these dear friends step immediately back
into ripples of their past:
early stages of psychoanalysis

social-political activism—Marie
arrested after the Anschluss, interrogated, let go.

Ma tells Marie for the first time how she escaped that arrest:
    ...hatte an diesem Abend Dienst und war daher nicht dabei.
    (... I had night duty and therefore was not there.)

At last, better times raising children,
what the grandchildren say and look like.
Keen clinicians, they each make fresh
observations about child development.

Back and forth they sign off:
    Ich habe solche Sehnsucht nach dir ... (I have such longing
    for you ...) Treffen wir uns in Wien ... (Let us meet
    in Vienna ...)

Marie's letters smell faintly of cigarettes
she never could put down
that eventually kill her,
before they ever meet again.

ALL OVER

Boxed, a hundred years of letters stack
into my shopping cart.

Blank shelves and walls stare,
a last wink of sun sparks across the Hudson River.
The tired apartment heaves a vast gush of stale air.

I turn the lock.
It shivers
for the last time

                              as the bolt drops.

Part II:

Crisscross Runways:
Kennedy/Schwechat/Kennedy

To Vienna

The shift feels sudden. Last swim at six p.m.
water dark, cold tang
on day-warmed
silk-soft rainwater.
I reminisce, walking with Ma—

eyesight failing, she leaned on a cane, turned me this way,
that way, one crooked narrow street after another,
in Vienna's old city:
>*There, see, the baker painted on the wall in Bäckerstrasse?*
Not so blind, I thought!

Next day, speed walk the route she walked to her
Gymnasium (high school)
—from 22 Lederergasse, where she lived until she
fled—downhill—
past the Rathaus—leap into Minoritenkirche (church):
See the exact copy in mosaic of Leonardo's Last Supper—after
a minute, *Come on!*
she pulls my arm—triple march—to Herrengasse 10—
we stand, look up—*there on the top floors was the
Schwarzwaldschule,
my Gymnasium.*

It's now the luxury Herrenhof Hotel.
I must go back. Walk with her ghost.

In May 2019, Karl Fallend's book, will be presented.
He writes of the astonishing treasure in his mailbox,
a fat envelope.
Inside, Ma and Marie's late letters.

Karl, trusted researcher, through his book will close the circle
of a 65-year friendship—

His research will open my circle—
he has found and connected me to Marie's
two daughters: Anna and Veronica.
Am I in a vortex?
Winter garden ice dissolves
emerald rain glistens.
Sap rises above long morning shadows

cardinal flits carnelian
above a burst
of gold forsythia.

Spring continues to crack the mirror of all conceit.

GAME OF PARTS

1.

We three daughters meet for the first time
in my apartment on Manhattan's Upper West Side.
Cloud-strewn afternoon pales the dining table
mango mousse cake, coffee *mit Schlag,* pace our conversation.

As if we have always known each other—
Vienna's ancestral tug.

We race through details of our mothers' story:
mine nicknamed Els, theirs, Mimi.
Together we search the photo we all have—
the lineup from their high school class play.

Mimi is the tallest one (like Anna and Veronica)
at the head, in gold pumps with a daring pageboy haircut.
My mother is fourth from the end, pensive,
her long braids coiled over her ears.

On the cusp of professional lives,
Anschluss menaced Death.
They fled. Lost connection with each other.

After forty years, accidentally find one other
at an International Psychoanalytic Congress in Vienna.

We delicately finger the tissue-thin, typewritten letters.
We can hear each other's hearts pumping, feel
our mothers' freed spirits,
the breath-beat of each sentence,

the pulse of Karl's book, which like a lightning rod
struck us together, sitting in a circle, daughters three,
agonizing, reprising, *Who are we?*

Veronica confides: *Our mother's last whisper: your Protestant*
    father was really a Jew.
Anna replies: *She never denied that **she** was Jewish. Her passions,*
    psychoanalysis and communism, were her true religions.
As for me, I pitch in: *My parents never hid their religious mix.*
Brought me up with the universal Golden Rule. But even
in postwar,
melting pot New York City, unspoken bigotry made
me vulnerable—
better to be 100% Jewish, or 100% Christian.

2.

Why must this history drill relentless into our first hellos?
My mind winds and twists. Ancestral figures
weave, push cake and coffee to the side.

My mother's strangled voice echoes:
> *Your grandmother Edith, Jewish enough for the Nazis.*
> *Not enough for the Red Cross or US Jewish agencies*
> *to help me rescue her.*

Grandma Edith chose suicide
over the gruesome cattle car ride,
after which to stagger with hundreds, naked, jammed into
the gas chamber—
> 20 minutes of hydrogen cyanide
> > Bloody mouths foaming,
> > > clawing for air
> > > > to die.

Spirit fingers fan cards across the table.
I seem to hear them hiss: *Now you shall have to play the
game, girls!*
> Anna in a trance hides the colored side:

Red card stands for Gypsy
Black for Aryan
Blue, this one Christian
Yellow means Hebrew/Jew.

She takes her turn, uncovers two:
> *I got yellow, yellow.*

Elisabeth Frischauf   117

I do not feel I am a Jew, but
if ever anyone attacks a Jew, for sure I am a Jew!

Veronica dreamlike sifts. *Yellow. Yellow! Me too?*
I do not identify as a Jew. But,
any slur or slap
for sure, I insist I am a Jew.

Last up, I'm drawn to yellow and blue.
Blue—am I Christian? Yellow, split/one half Jew/in two?
Attack
any Jew, then
I declare myself a Jew!

3.

Plates, forks, cups clatter as we stand to clear the table.
I tell them my mother, would proclaim:
Instead of having a religion, Hitler marked us as a **race.**
Anna's eyebrows arc. Veronica's eyes jump.
Under the Black Third Reich, my mother, furious, explained,
with one drop of Jewish blood, we infected, like cancer,
the pure Aryan German.

We became vermin to **fumigate.**

How can we daughters three just be?
Jew-Jew-less-Jew-ess-es?
Can't we demand:
CONSIDER ME?

4.

New World daughters three,
light our winter solstice Christmas tree.
Cherish ancestors who kept Shabbat
and those who sat in church on Sunday.

We know
in this world
    when there is light and day and night
    when there is fog, rain, and night
    when there is word and thought, there is a need
    to draw lines,
      count, divide, one-half, quarter, eighth, sixteenth

Go ahead. Claim us.
If you can claim
    hymn, ode, sonnet, young, old, new
    whole, half, quarter, or sixteenth note,
    WE are claimable.
We are Adagio, Andante, Rest.
    Allegro, Rondo cantabile, to the end,
    to the beginning ...

Elisabeth Frischauf   119

Boxes

Wing-side seat, airplane engine roar.
Lullabies, clouds, ashes, remains
on the way to Vienna, far away.

Memory mind-box—what was never said.
   Who-is-it photos. Box closes.

An other box, an other loss.
Stinking, ever-present loss!
Soil, bones, ashes.

Another box, an un-do box, wreathed
in net, snagged on deep ocean crag.
Haul 'er up! Sides splay,
corners gush water. Free,

my soul, with their souls, fly Home.
A bower a-bove the clouds.
                Love-lulling-lullabies explode.

Hail the 1st of May 2019

Austria's flag billows
red-white-red exuberant.
Balconies, poles, fanned
by Vindobona's steady good wind
that blesses wine grapes
as the Romans discovered
so long ago.

Rotes (Red) Wien is all out
on the sun-splashed Rathausplatz.

Das rote Wien 1919–1934(Red Vienna, 1919–1934), a
historical exhibit
of the brief post-World War I hegemony of socialism, before
the right-wing *Putsch*
and eventually Anschluss.

A luxury tax funds public housing
for millions of homeless refugees
gathered from the smashed Austro-Hungarian Empire, the
blind, leg-less, shellshocked soldiers
gasping from gassed lungs.

1920s the small modern apartment is born:
efficiency kitchen, communal laundry room
around central open space with health clinic,
kindergarten, community classrooms.

I step back into this creative ferment.
There, my great-aunt Mitzi who pioneered sex education, and

my enthusiastic young, yet-to-be mother, her
beloved, committed Gymnasium teacher, Aline Furtmüller,
her ambitious future anatomy professor,
Julius Tandler, her excited
friends organized into youth groups

build, study, rally by day
oceans of coffee, hot debates all night:
Wie leben? (How to live?)
continued into university,
this social experiment
sprung
from the shattered shards.

No wonder Ma's chronic nostalgia never gave out!

MAY FIFTH

I suckle lilac scent
tender my skin with baby linden leaves
white-rose chestnut tree blossoms feather my bones.
Great gyres radiate from the Stephansdom's magnetic spire

a slice of *Mozarttorte*—marzipan, pistachio, praline,
chocolate and

down the Café Korb stairs I go
    into the café's meeting room
        for Karl's book presentation with
           Ma and Marie's letters,
where Freud
held his Wednesday evening discussions
where Grandfather Martin and Great-Uncle Hermann
                participated and now I.

MOTHER'S DAY, MAY 12, 2019

You will cleave the white-stuccoed church nestled in a
mossy rock cleft,
its settled green onion-spire contemplating thin tenuous air

You will love the absolute availability of picture
postcard scenery—
liquid turquoise Fuschlsee, rimmed by helter-skelter,
snowy peaks
this mid-May, Mother's Day

You will try to ingest rows of neat marzipan-filled Mozart
chocolate balls in Salzburg, your mother's birth city

You will keep the view: medieval stone fortress, crowning
the city and below the thrusting Salzach River's icy gray-green,
the color of your mother's eyes

You will infuse urgent lungful upon lungful of clear
mountain air
in your stay here, yet you must return to the great
Atlantic's thick
salty, where your children and grandchildren play

You will enter the white-walled baroque church with
the freshly
gilded Madonna holding her important baby and even though
you do not believe in miracles

You will light a candle in front of her, to the clink of
50 euro cents
in the locked black box

You will tell her you need a granddaughter to replace
the one you lost before she could draw breath
and ask that your poems sail forth

You will seep organ music into your soul as it booms into
the vault of heaven and the nuns chant evensong
in steady soprano plainsong. You will chant along.

You will leave the church as 6 o'clock Angelus bells bounce
over red roof tiles and cobblestones with their inset brass
memorial *Stolpersteine* aglow—
etched names: Rose, Hannah, Moshe, ringing:
er–r–r–rinnere, r–remember us

You will see the evening sun lie over new-grass green surge up
low-lying slopes, the cows' steadfast plod to feast
in blooming meadows

Elisabeth Frischauf   125

Yes, you love this Austria with the light luff of horror
on your skin—
Hitler's steely-eyed hatred bulging over the countryside stolen
from you when your parents had to flee

You are the envelope written on both sides.
Double-fold complete
in this seventh decade when leaves loosen and the vine
begins to dry.

You will try and try to keep this homeland, but like a teardrop
caught in a spider's web, an unceremonious wind flings it away.

GOODBYE, DANUBE RIVER

Three-point windmill spins
spear-shaft over Danube's fast flow,
gray-green speckled
like a dashing trout. Not so blue like in the famous song
Ma used to sing!

You who pass centuries of death-blood
and madness
    Do you waltz, I don't care anymore—Did you ever?

RETURN TO THE LANDHAUS

May 22, Ma's birthday.
The garden hung with scent,
lily of the valley, her favorite flower
waited, as it must, to bloom.

I return to mother.
To warm earth, grass
refusing silence.

I lie naked, sag-breast, slack-belly,
meld into fresh-mown clover, my
inside/outside one.

I return to these letters
at 72, ready at last.
I will organize, sort, scan

I, who still carry the terror will
write, shout!

Eight pages catch my eye—
Ma, at 72, begins in English:
    Some of my experiences and feelings will die with me . . .

I loved Vienna, really like a person. The city of laughter
and tears,
of old and new beauty.

Thinking about my life . . . There was a lot of emotional
suffering and pain and a lot of physical illnesses,
but the joy prevailed.

On page seven, she must switch to German,
just as I had to
when she and Pa died.
    Denk so viel an die Eltern, (I think so much about
    my parents)
    she writes and I think the same with her.

If only Ma had told me
how the murder, suicide, genocide
that curated her life
began to ebb.

Can it be, if you live long enough
the Holocaust loses its stranglehold and fades?

We flowed between two languages,
translated ourselves along the way.
My every fiber soaked with you
I must go ahead with **my** flow.

I, who still carry the terror must
WRITE
          SUMMON
                    WAKE UP

A river will out. You can't contain it

                    A poem will out

                              You can't restrain it.

LATER

I sit in the *Landhaus*
behind heavily curtained windows,
another record-splitting heat wave—
the lake boils, sears my hand, my hot heart.

I, who still carry the terror, must ask,
Do we forget last century's Nazi mechanized Final
Solution to exterminate:
Jews, Gypsies, dissidents, "degenerates" Jehovah's
Witnesses, priests, Slavs . . .
starved, tortured,
shot and piled into pits?
In Auschwitz, 6,000 Jews gassed every hour
easily 18–20,000,000 murders, all together?

My Grandson Waits

in the garden for morning sun.
A crow calls:
>*Fly on today's wind*
>>*Swim on the lip of the universe*

Then, eyes darting from face to face, lands on the table.
>*Hey, Grandma, she's tooken your toast!*

Grandmother land.
American-born children, grandchildren, and I,
alive to hold their hands

The truth is out.
>>>>>You cannot tame it.

ACKNOWLEDGMENTS

1. Page 4: Frischauf, Hermann, "Die Fragmente" ("The Fragments) with my translation in *Des Lebens Tausendfältige Gestalt* (*Life's Thousand Facets*) p. 122, Europäischer Verlag, Vienna 1962

2. Pages 5, 9,10: Pappenheim-Frischauf, Marie, "Lager Gurs, Juni1940" ("Camp Gurs, June 1940") p. 51 and "Aufwachen bei Nacht, März 1943" (Waking up at Night, March 1943") p. 60, my translations in *Verspätete Ernte, Zerstreuter Saat (Late Harvest, Scattered Seeds)*, Europäischer Verlag, Vienna 1962

3. Pages 58, 67, 74: Fallend, Karl, *Mimi und Els, Stationen einer Freundschaft (Stages of a Friendship)*, Loecker Verlag, Vienna 2019. Within this book are copies of the original correspondence in German between my mother and Marie Langer.

4. Langer Marie, *Von Wien bis Managua. Wege einer Psychoanalytikerin*, Friburgo 1986

5. Handlbauer, Bernhard, *Hölderlin, Feuchtersleben, Freud, Beitrage zur Geschichte der Psychoanalyse, der Psychiatrie und zur Neurologie*, Nausner & Nausner, Graz 2004. Contains much history pertaining to my family, my mother's original writings in German, and many of her scientific papers and other writings translated by her with my father from English to German.

6. Konstantin Kaiser for editing and publishing the first
    bilingual edition: Frischauf, Elisabeth, *They Clasp
    My Hand/Die meine Hand ergreifen, Gedichte,/Poems*,
    Theodor Kramer Gesellschaft, Vienna, 2022
7. The entire Prologue first appeared translated to
    German in the journal, Zwischenwelt Nr.2/2021, S.
    20-26, September 2021
8. Earlier versions published of "My Holocaust"
    and "First Generation American," in English,
    Geteilte Erinnerung (Shared Memory), pp151-155
    Czernin Verlag, Vienna 2004
9. Ernst Karner, my translator for the bilingual edition
10. Patricia Brody for editing the English-language
    manuscript
11. The city of Vienna and the Culture Ministry of the
    Republic of Austria for travel stipends and support of
    the original bilingual edition
12. Carlos Passi for photographing my mixed media
    ceramic hand for the front cover

Traditional and contemporary form bring **Frischauf**'s voice to life in today's world of disrupted interpersonal relationships from the long trail of refugee trauma (her family's experience of the Holocaust) as well as modern social upheaval in traditional family and women's roles.

Her epic narrative memoir poem, They Clasp My Hand, short-listed for the Austria Literary Prize, was published in April 2022. Appearing as a bilingual, English/German edition from Theodor Kramer Verlag, Vienna, Austria, Edmund de Waal, author of "The Hare with the Amber Eyes," comments: ". . . a wonderful book of poems. I am finding such resonance and recognition with them."

She was born in 1947 on the Upper West Side of Manhattan, where her parents married and settled to raise a family. Her mother (Else Pappenheim-Frischauf) fled Austria shortly after Anschluss in the midst of psychoanalytic training. Her father completed his last year of high school in Vienna under the Nazi regime and then fled.

Frischauf is herself a psychiatrist and an active visual artist in many media: ceramics, collage, mobiles. "Writing poetry is intimately bound up with my artwork. These many avenues allow me to convey my personal perspective to the world I live in. The playful side of me emerges, my love of storytelling, but also serious social commentary.

Being multilingual and anchored in two cultures—the family homeland in Austria and New York City— enriches everything I do."

Two more volumes of memoir verse are in the publication pipeline creating a trilogy together with *They Clasp My Hand*.

She lives on a small plot of land in Putnam County, New York.

* 9 7 9 8 9 9 0 8 0 0 9 0 8 *